D0392737

RESISTANCE

I, WITNESS

RESISTANCE

My Story of Activism

FRANTZY LUZINCOURT

Norton Young Readers

An Imprint of W. W. Norton & Company
Independent Publishers Since 1923

Series edited by Zainab Nasrati, Zoe Rosenblum, Amanda Uhle, and Dave Eggers.
[copyright TK]

Learn to do right; seek justice.
Defend the oppressed.

—Isaiah 1:17

All power to the people.

—

CONTENTS

INTRODUCTION

Zainab Nasrati, Amanda Uhle, and Dave Eggers

One of the best ways to understand a complicated moment in history is to read the story of someone who lived through it. That's what this series is all about: letting young people—who experienced recent world events firsthand—tell their stories. Our hope is that by hearing one person's story, our readers will learn about others' struggles and think of ways we might make the world more peaceful and equitable.

Teenagers like Malala Yousafzai and Greta Thunberg became iconic for standing up for what they believe is right. Other teens, not yet as well known, have also stepped up to make a difference. When Adama Bah was a teenager in post-9/11 New York, she was falsely accused of being a terrorist simply because she is Muslim. She spoke up to defend herself and others like her. When Salvador Gómez-Colón was fifteen, his family endured Hurricane Maria in Puerto Rico. Using his deep local knowledge and incredible dedication to helping his neighbors, Salvador founded Light & Hope for Puerto Rico, raising money and gathering supplies to help islanders with basic needs during the emergency.

The I, Witness books bring you stories of young people like you who have faced extraordinary challenges in their lives. Their stories are exciting and surprising, filled with struggle—and humor and joy, too. We hope that you'll consider your own life and your own story as you read. Is there a problem in the world or in your life that you'd like to help solve?

In this book, you'll meet Frantzy Luzincourt, who was born in New York City to parents who were Haitian immigrants. He faced racial profiling and other discrimination as he grew up. The unfair and traumatic experiences of Black Americans were especially noticeable to Frantzy as he transitioned between his neighborhood, whose residents were largely Caribbean immigrants, and his private high school, which was mostly white and privileged.

He was inspired and supported by several teachers in his life, including Mr. Blackmon, who helped Frantzy start a Black Student Union at his high school, the first of many leadership positions Frantzy has held as a youth activist. After the murder of George Floyd in 2020, Frantzy cofounded Strategy for Black Lives, an award-winning youth-led organization that fights for Black Americans' civil rights. Many of us will recognize the challenges Frantzy has faced, and all of us will be moved by his resolve and tenacity in the face of discrimination. As readers ourselves we were heartened and inspired by Frantzy's story, and we hope you will be, too.

RESISTANCE

CHAPTER 1

Icon

The day was not going the way I had planned. I ran through the airport as fast as I could, but it didn't matter. I'd missed my flight to San Francisco. I'd taken a bus and a train to the Port Authority, then a shuttle to Newark Liberty International Airport. Basically, the journey from Flatbush to the airport was more than an hour and a half long.

This is going to be a very long day, I thought. Luckily the airline staff was able to get me on the next flight, but it meant my time in San Francisco would be even more limited than it already was. It would mean arriving at my hotel late, going to the International Congress of Youth Voices conference the next day, and then heading straight back to New York City the day after that.

The 2018 International Congress of Youth Voices was a new conference for young writers and activists. This was my first time traveling alone and my first time attending a conference. I was hoping to make myself known. I applied for the event with an essay about using hip-hop as a learning tool in the classroom. I called the essay "Hip Hop Pedagogy: From the Booth to the Classroom." I also cited my work building my high school's first-ever Black Student Union and my work with youth-led IntegrateNYC, a nonprofit combatting school segregation in New York City, where it is a really big problem. Education equity is a strong motivating force for me and the work I do.

When I finally arrived at the airport in San Francisco, I called an Uber. I tend to keep my cool in stressful situations, but after that day I learned that I do not like missing planes at all.

But now the driver sailed along the highway, and I could finally relax.

I used the key card to let myself into my hotel room, set my bag down, and began cleaning myself up after the long day of traveling. I came to this gathering to learn about different perspectives, to grow and become more open-minded. My personal goal was to become more strategic in how I build relationships with activists and other people across the world.

My phone began to buzz. It was Amanda, who was organizing the event, and she had a question for me:

"How would you feel about introducing Representative John Lewis tomorrow?

The question took me by surprise.

"I think you two are aligned in your work, and you'd be great," she added.

"Sure. Absolutely," I said, without fully grasping the great privilege being offered to me.

I didn't really comprehend that I'd be introducing John Lewis the person. I knew him as a figure, but John Lewis as a person giving a speech at a conference that I was attending did not quite make sense to me. It hadn't sunk in.

I remember thinking later, *What a great opportunity to speak to this new congress, to a bunch of youth activists. I'll be able to stand out and participate, and not just fade into the background.* But, as I settled into my hotel room, it began to hit me. I would be introducing *the* John Lewis at tomorrow's youth congress.

The following evening, the attendants of the first International Congress of Youth Voices boarded a boat and sailed into the San Francisco Bay. As the boat softly rocked beneath us and the breeze blew gently on our young and shamelessly hopeful faces, I stood up in front of activists my age from around the world and read from some prepared notes.

"In the modern era, there are only a few people that can accurately be referred to as a living legend. John Lewis is one of them."

As I spoke, the gravity of the moment and

my role in it hit me further. I, Frantzy Luzincourt, the twenty-year-old son of Haitian
immigrants from East Flatbush, New York,
was introducing the great civil rights icon
John Lewis. John Lewis, elected to the House
of Representatives seventeen consecutive
times. John Lewis, one of the original thirteen
Freedom Riders. John Lewis, who marched
alongside Dr. King in Selma at about the
same age as I am now.

"Be leaders," he instructed us. "Lead the
way, get in trouble, good trouble. You can
help redeem our world. Save our planet."

I return to that moment in my head a lot.
When he passed, I was trying my best to make
good trouble every day. I was about ten times

more active in my civil rights work than I had been when I first met him on that day when I gave the introduction. John Lewis inspired so many people, including me. It's time for our generation to continue to pave the way. Amanda was right. We are aligned. Since that evening on the boat, his words have only become more and more true.

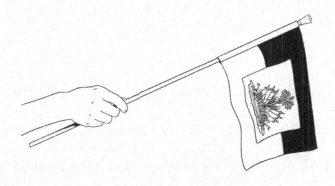

CHAPTER 2

Voice

The part of Brooklyn where I live and grew up, between East Flatbush and Canarsie, is very heavily immigrant in composition, much like most of New York City. We're a very diverse city. My neighborhood is made up of people from Jamaica, Haiti, Trinidad, Guyana, Bajan, and Barbados. Brooklyn is where the most Caribbeans live, outside of the Caribbean itself. Our streets are filled with the sounds of dancehall, reggae, and kompa. And with the smell of jerk chicken: the Jamaican restaurants cook it in humongous grove barrels on our neighborhood blocks.

There are a lot of houses, but there are also a lot of project developments. I am fortunate enough to have grown up in and to now live in a house. I am a first-generation American born to Haitian immigrants. Anything we ever need pertaining to Haiti is available because there's such a large, vibrant Haitian community here. Living in East Flatbush and

Canarsie has really helped me maintain a connection to my culture.

From kindergarten to eighth grade, I went to a Catholic school in my own neighborhood. I was surrounded by Black students and other people of color. During that time, my mother worked as a respiratory therapist and often stayed at the hospital from seven a.m to eight p.m., after waking up at four a.m. for work. My father also worked long hours, until he got into a bad accident and went on disability. Throughout my childhood and into my middle school years, the libraries of Canarsie became headquarters for my older brother and me after school. It was the place where my parents felt we, as kids, could stay safely without having to rely on paying for a babysitter.

My parents always made it clear that education came before all else. As for many children of immigrants, there was a lot of pressure on my siblings and me to excel academically. We were not allowed to partake in any social pleasure or entertainments on school days and we received rewards—or punishments—based on our academic performance.

But sometimes I just didn't want to do my schoolwork. Reading was one of the only leisure activities that was acceptable to my parents whenever, wherever. If I didn't want to do my homework, I could just read books like the Harry Potter, Divergent, and Percy Jackson series. My appetite for books was super-huge and the library became my spot. Spending so much time there after school worked out well for me. It made me an avid reader.

In sixth grade, while I was reading scripture out loud in my religion class, my teacher, Mrs. Dupre, stopped me.

"I enjoy the way you read scripture, Frantzy," she said. "Have you ever considered trying out for the oratory competition?"

I knew I was very good at reading out loud, but I had never considered public speaking or oratory as part of it. She wanted me to represent my school in a competition for middle schoolers in the Brooklyn and Queens Catholic diocese.

"No," I said.

The idea made me nervous. I didn't think I had what it took to recite speeches in front of people. I could read scripture out loud in a class full of people I knew, but in front of strangers? In a competition? That part made me uncomfortable—I wasn't sure how I would like that. I'd done a lot of martial arts competitions through my childhood, and those competitions were in front of strangers, but martial arts were something I actively enjoyed and pursued.

"I see this in you," she said.

I didn't see it at that time. Why would I jump on an opportunity that I felt unsure about?

But Mrs. Dupre did not let up. The next year, she brought it up with me again. This time she was a little more forceful.

"You should do it," she said.

Looking at her, I was unable to say no a second time. I didn't know how to. *Okay*, I thought. *She's my favorite teacher. We're pretty cool. I'll take a chance.*

Public speaking is the number one phobia in the United States, but it turns out I have no problems speaking in front of a crowd about anything. I am just really good at public speaking. I ended up going to the oratory finals in both seventh and eighth grade. I believe my time in the library is the reason. All that time reading was the way I found my voice. It made me comfortable enough to speak, to write speeches, and to represent the school and win competitions. There's no way I would have been recognized or approached as a leader in any shape or form if I had not developed those skills. Reading empowered me.

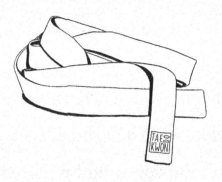

CHAPTER 3

Profiled

My entire middle school life centered on about six square blocks. When I wasn't in the library after school, I was three blocks away at the dojo practicing tae kwon do.

One day, when I was about ten years old, my mother picked me up from tae kwon do. It was one of her days off and she was going to take me to the deli across the street for a snack before we headed home.

We left the dojo, and I removed my belt, folded it up, and tucked it into my jacket pocket. We have a rule in martial arts that you don't wear your belt in public. You only wear it in the dojo, even if you just need to run across the street. The belt was bulky in my pocket, but I didn't think anything of it.

We walked around the deli looking at the meats and breads and chips. It was nothing special. Just an average deli, and we were just going about our day. But the owner was eyeing me. Eyeing my bulky jacket pocket.

As my mother paid, the owner glared at me.

"Show me what's in your pocket," he ordered.

"What are you talking about?" my mother asked.

The man was still eyeing my pocket.

"I'm not stealing, it's my belt," I said.

A look of anger flashed across my mother's face. I began to pull my belt from my pocket, but my mother stopped me.

"Don't empty your pockets," she instructed. "That is not necessary."

The deli owner assumed that I was stealing a fifty-cent bag of chips. It was ridiculous. We marched right out of there. My mother was furious.

My brother had also been profiled on the

very same street. He was just going about his day, leaving the dojo, when the cops detained him. The cause for his arrest was their usual story from the beginning of time: You look like someone who has been doing something illegal. He wasn't, and he was eventually let go. But these two incidents have stuck with me. My mother's anger on that day is clear in my mind.

BSU MEETING
TONIGHT!

CHAPTER 4

President

The first time I was thrown into an environment that was predominantly white was high school. I went to a school for the gifted—for high-performing students—that used screening for admissions. You had to have a certain grade-point average to get in. Because of socioeconomic disparities, going to a good school, let alone a gifted one in New York City, generally means it is ninety-nine percent white, and this one was an hour-and-a-half commute for me. It was in Manhattan Beach, a Jewish neighborhood in Brooklyn— very rich and very white.

The transition was stark. My classmates had been in the public school system and had already taken algebra and geometry. I didn't have any of that. They also had knowledge that I didn't have of how the system worked. I didn't know about state tests. I didn't know about talking to counselors or ordering transcripts.

Before high school, I experienced microaggressions when I was out in public, but now I was experiencing them in a school setting. White kids would say things like: Why do you talk white? Generally, I'd ignore those comments, but they added up. So in this school, the Black students and students of color stuck together. We watched out for one another.

My favorite teacher at this time was Mr. Maurice Blackmon. He taught English. He was a slim Black man on the shorter side who dressed kind of preppy. The thing about him was he was new, and he was young. He was able to connect with students a lot easier. He was closer to us in age. He taught in a very colloquial way. He was able to make the class laugh.

He was very social-justice-minded and introduced us to books like *Animal Farm*. He was intent on starting the school's first Black Student Union. As a teacher, he naturally wanted us to be invested in our futures. A lot of times students of color get left behind, but he went out of his way to create a welcoming and safe space for us.

From the get-go, he had his eyes on me for the Black Student Union. When he initially approached me with the idea of starting it, I was very hesitant. I brushed it off, pushed it away. For the second time in my life a teacher was asking me to do something and I was hesitant. At the time, I wasn't comfortable being in the public eye regarding race and politics. I wasn't confident in taking a stand and publicly fighting for racial equity in my school. I didn't necessarily believe I was the best person to champion such causes.

But Mr. Blackmon was persistent. He brought it up constantly. I saw him in class every day. I couldn't hide from him. If I had questions about a class project, he'd bring up the union. If I was coming by his office to get my grade on something, he'd bring up the union. Eventually, I just pulled up, because, why not? At the end of the day, I was currying favor with a teacher who was going to give me my grade. I decided I might as well see what the union could be about.

Once Mr. Blackmon convinced me to join the Black Student Union, it meant he had my friends, too. As Black students and students of color, we did everything together. It was a survival mechanism in such a white environment. If there were only five black guys, and we were friends, if one of us went to an after-school activity, we were all going to, because we all traveled home together anyway. We figured we might as well do everything together, or at least do most things together, because we were not going to leave anyone behind.

The next thing I knew, Mr. Blackmon was asking me to be president.

New York City is very diverse, but we're also very segregated. Every neighborhood has its own people. If you are white and growing up in a predominantly white neighborhood and going to a predominantly white school, you seldom interact with Black people and other cultures. I was worried about how my white schoolmates would react to a Black Student Union.

But I wanted to live up to Mr. Blackmon's standards. I didn't want to let him down. His strong confidence and faith in my abilities changed my mind about being president. I began to look forward to taking on this role and seeing where it could go. He believed it would be a good thing for me. I trusted him and that he had my best interests at heart.

Many of the white kids didn't know what to make of the Black Student Union, as I'd anticipated. During school announcements when they called my name as the president, kids in the classroom looked at me differently. Some chuckled, others seemed annoyed. They seemed to say: *What is that?* I would be walking through the hallways just as a regular student, and kids would call to me, teasing me a little bit:

Oh, what is the Black Student Union? Are

you the president of the world of Blacks now? What are you going to do? Are you trying to bother white people? Is there going to be a White Student Union?

It was annoying. But it never really fazed me. I knew they were misguided and ignorant. I just had to do what I needed to do to educate my campus and help my community.

We had a lot of work. We organized workshops and learning opportunities. We brought in professors and scholars and discussed the *n*-word and its use in popular culture. We established our school's first-ever Martin Luther King Jr. assembly, putting on a play about racism and his legacy. We regularly put on social functions demonstrating Black excellence and led workshops discussing subjects like police brutality. We also pointed our efforts toward school policy and the administration. We met with the teachers' union and the principal to make sure that teachers were giving Black students attention and consideration on campus. We made sure we were advancing policy reform as well. We did a lot of work within the high school to make sure that future Black students would have better experiences than we had.

As time went on, other students started to see how serious and committed I was and how the union was going to fight for this change whether they supported us or not. White students would come up to me and say: I understand where you're coming from now. I apologize for how I acted before. Your performance and what you guys did was amazing. I learned a lot. Students started to respect me and applaud me. Respect and admiration replaced the mockery that I had received before when my name was first announced over that loudspeaker as president of the Black Student Union. A change had come to our school.

Mr. Blackmon pushed me in high school to help me find my voice as an activist, especially when it came to civil rights protests and being African American. I'm still doing the same leadership work that he inspired me to do when I was only fifteen years old. The Black

Student Union and being its president really activated my potential. It started a domino effect in my life that propelled me forward into larger roles as an activist and organizer.

CHAPTER 5

Gala

College was a whole new world for me. All of a sudden I had a lot more autonomy to pursue the interests that moved me. My course load wasn't being dictated to me in the same way it had been in high school. And once again, much like in middle school, I found myself in a diverse environment. In fact, I was attending one of the most diverse schools in the state. My campus community spoke more languages than any other in the country.

I decided to attend City College of New York for two specific reasons. First, it was affordable. Because of my family's socioeconomic background, Ivy Leagues and private schools just weren't plausible. I applied to Howard University, and I got a really good scholarship, but it still just wasn't monetarily feasible even with the scholarship. Second, I knew that the Macaulay Honors Program at CUNY/City College would put me on a path toward my ultimate goal: law school.

Ever since I was in the seventh grade, I'd

wanted to become an attorney. At that time, my math teacher told my parents during a parent/ teacher conference that I was a troublemaker in class. She was like, "Yeah, he's a good kid, but he's always getting involved and causing problems and inserting himself in situations." She continued, "He should probably become a lawyer. Hardy-har-har." When my parents told me about this, I couldn't say for certain if she was being serious, but I took her words at face value. Ever since then, I haven't really looked back. As I've gotten older, I've only become more committed to the idea.

The Macaulay Honors Program at City College basically gives you a full ride for all four years. They gave me a laptop. I got to pick all my classes before other students chose theirs. Those of us in the program had a special counselor and a bunch of opportunities to go to museums and cultural programs for free. I would not have to pay anything for my undergrad education. I'm the youngest child and my parents had already put my brother through college, which was a financial strain. I thought, *Hey, this is not only a win for my future, but also a win for my family, because Lord knows my parents are probably worried about sending another kid to college.*

City College also had the Colin Powell School for Civic and Global Leadership, which was right up my alley. It had a really strong program in public policy, international relations, and political science. It also had a fellowship for public service, and a fellowship for students who wanted to go to law school. I basically had everything I wanted and was interested in. Plus, it was in Harlem, which is far from Flatbush/Canarsie. Because I wasn't getting the experience of going out of town or out of state to attend college, I enjoyed having a whole different part of the city to explore.

Mr. Blackmon's wisdom and guidance taught me how to take opportunities. So the first week of college, I went to the student government office to ask them how to get involved. I ran for student government my freshman year. I lost, but I trusted the process and didn't fight the results. I ran again my spring of sophomore year, and I won. I was elected to serve as a senator representing the College of Liberal Arts and Sciences starting the following academic year. Eventually I worked my way up to president.

I took the lessons of starting the first-ever Black Student Union in my high school and employed them on a grander scale in college. Much like when I planned the inaugural Martin Luther King Day event for the Black Student Union, when I was president of the City College student body, one of the biggest agenda items on my plate was City College's first-ever Black History Month gala.

The idea started with the Black Student Caucus. A lot of the Black folks in student government also had leadership positions in other Black organizations. We formed the idea together. Student government was the body that could organize all the details of a gala and assume the most logistical burden because we had the institutional power and money behind us.

Planning a Martin Luther King Day event is one thing, but when it comes to planning a gala, it's a whole other animal. We had to worry about tickets and attendance, food, guest speakers, security. It was a lot. It was definitely logistically challenging.

But it was a humongous success.

The entire City College Black community was there. State Assemblyman for Harlem

Al Taylor gave a speech. He's my guy. The African Student Union did a dance. All live music and limbs swinging. A friend of mine who made music and rapped performed. It felt so good to give him that opportunity. It felt good to give all the Black performers at City College this venue to shine. It was beautiful. There was just a feeling of community and joy vibrating throughout the hall. And people were dressed, sparkling in tuxedos and gowns. Toward the end of the evening my executive vice president gave a champagne toast—though it was actually sparkling apple cider.

It was definitely a highlight of college for me and certainly a highlight of my time as president. I was on cloud nine with that achievement, but that didn't last long. Two weeks later, students began coming into my office with concerns. There was an illness spreading throughout the globe and they were scared.

I was the first person from CUNY student government to publicly call for the closing of schools because of the Covid-19 pandemic. With all the anxious students coming to our offices, I realized there was no other option. We kicked into action swiftly. I spent that time right before everything shut down helping design the reopening plan and shifting classes to a virtual platform. And, very importantly, I helped design a plan to keep the City College food pantry open so that our most vulnerable populations would still have access to food. I anticipated the Covid-19 situation would get much worse. I was right.

I graduated from college later that spring, during the worst pandemic in a century, while campus was still closed. As president, I potentially would have been able to give remarks from the stage at my graduation, which would have made my parents so proud. Instead, our graduation was done online, like most things that semester. I was sorry to miss the in-person ceremony but still proud of all I'd accomplished in my college career.

CHAPTER 6

Strategy

May 26, 2020, was the day Strategy for Black Lives was born. A group of my friends and one of my fraternity brothers were having a BBQ in Canarsie to celebrate Memorial Day. It was also my fraternity brother and best friend Jaret's birthday. We had a big menu. We were grilling chicken, burgers, and hot dogs. We had salad and a solid macaroni and cheese. It was the first social hangout I'd been to since the beginning of the coronavirus pandemic. We were all outside and still social distancing.

My friend Patrick was watching a video on his phone and I could tell it was upsetting him.

"Yo, have you seen this?" he asked, pointing the screen toward me. The police had murdered another Black man. I watched a few seconds and pushed the phone away.

"I'm good off that, man," I said. "How is this still happening?" I asked without expecting an answer. I'd seen these kinds of videos over and over again. Patrick and I had gone to marches and actions in high school. We went to our first protest, which was sparked by the killing of Eric Garner, when we were fifteen. I was pissed off, but that doesn't really capture the numbing mixture of anger and fear that I felt and that I continue to feel.

How is it that when I was in high school, six years prior, I was protesting against police brutality and fighting for Black Lives—and now I was a fully grown adult, had graduated from college, and I still had to protest for the same issues? What had we been doing these past six years?

Patrick is my best friend. We have been

best friends since middle school. While I was standing there with him at the BBQ, almost uncontainable rage and frustration was building up in me. *Enough is enough*, I thought. The two of us had a conversation. Why weren't we seeing structural or policy change? We knew we had to do something about this. We might not be able to solve the entire problem, but we were positive we could be a part of the solution. And I said, "I'll post on Instagram right now." I went on Instagram and created a story that basically said: If anyone is interested in doing something, a response to what's been going on, swipe up and DM me. Every person who reached out to me, I put in a group chat. And that evening we planned to have an emergency Zoom call to discuss what had been going on and to develop a response. I posted a Zoom link on my Twitter account announcing the time of the meeting.

That was a mistake. My Twitter account was public. That night a group of us spoke over Zoom and began designing our seven-point document of demands. As we were discussing our plans, two or three white supremacists joined the call and started hurling the *n*-word at us.

It was very upsetting, but it also confirmed something. I texted Patrick: *Yo. If this is our first*

FRANTZY LUZINCOURT

ever call and we already got white supremacists trying to stop us, that means we must be doing something right. We must be on the right path.

After the attack by those internet racists, we created the seven-point document of demands. We sent it to every media outlet we could find.

1. **The Implementation of a Policy That Would Penalize Those Who Falsely Call the Police.**

    Those who waste police resources on calls that do not involve violations of law and/or are racially charged will face consequences.

56

2. **An Assembly with the NYPD Commissioner and the Mayor of New York City.**

   Direct communication lowers the possibility of misunderstanding.

3. **The Elimination of the "Blue Wall of Silence."**

   Encouraging the dismantlement of this "wall" will improve transparency, indicate areas of improvement, and ensure that police officers are held accountable for their actions.

4. **The Appointment of an Independent Inspector General.**

   Through this appointment, further

oversight of police policies and behavior can be accomplished.

5. **The Revision of the Vetting Process for Police Officers.**
Toughening up the vetting process for police officers will help ensure only people who are devoted to protecting and serving our communities can wear the badge.

6. **The Commitment of Elected Prosecutors of New York to Hold Police Accountable.**
Elected prosecutors should be at the forefront of holding law enforcement accountable for their actions.

7. **The Community Must Be Involved in Ensuring Their Own Safety**

Community members must be able to hold law enforcement accountable and must be included in the criminal justice process.

The following day, we were invited to a news conference on live TV where we explained our demands.

CHAPTER 7

Protest

It is very hard to start an organization. It is a headache. I am lucky to have started Strategy for Black Lives with two people I know and trust: my best friend Patrick and Timothy, whom I know from organizing together as student leaders with the City University of New York. I am so glad to have had these men by my side, but in the beginning stages of the organization it felt like we were building the plane as we were flying it. The movement was so fast-paced. Everything was response, response, response. We were trying to build an organization while fighting for our rights on the streets and at actions.

Two days after our Zoom call, Tim and I went to the infamous Barclays protest on a whim. The protest was a response to the viral video of George Floyd's murder by Derek Chauvin. Strategy for Black Lives was just beginning; we didn't have a presence yet. We didn't have an internet page or anything. As we marched, we saw firsthand how chaotic it was. There wasn't really any strategy. There was a lot of unorganized energy all around us. At one point, we came upon a random group of anarchist types. They were flipping over bikes and traffic cones. It felt like the narrative was getting twisted. We stopped and asked them: How does that honor and bring attention to the memory of George Floyd?

They didn't have an answer for us.

The event progressed into the evening and became more hectic and chaotic. People were throwing stuff at cops and setting cop cars on fire. Tim was trying to protect people from police who were behaving violently toward protesters but then the cops started pepper-spraying us. We were being pepper-sprayed just for trying to help people. People around us were crying and yelling and chanting. State senators and assembly people were getting pepper-sprayed and beaten up by the NYPD. I was right in the middle of the mayhem but felt detached and in shock. I didn't have a very emotional response. I was watching it unfold and learning from everything happening around me.

That's when I realized that it was our duty to participate in the movement and help preserve the integrity of it. What was playing out wasn't necessarily centering the movement's narrative. Tim and I took that back to our team. We needed to be strategic in a way that forced those in power to act. If we let the message get diluted, we were certainly going to lose the battle.

We weren't the kind of people who always wanted to lead marches. We preferred to support and empower people who were already doing the work on the ground. We started attending protests and introducing ourselves to the organizers and saying: Hey, we're Strategy for Black Lives, a young group from the neighborhood in New York City. Let us know how we can help. We began forming coalitions with other organizations. Making a reputation for our organization. And while we were in the field, we made sure the protests were going on and going well.

We built a protest formula of sorts. We'd

have people in positions—two people in the front of the crowd, two in the back, and two each on the right and left sides. They would monitor the actions, making sure everything was going well. Everyone would wear a black shirt and a yellow bandanna. If we saw cops or anything going wrong, we texted with each other. If we saw people going crazy or any chaos happening, we pivoted: *Yo, let's try to do things a different way.* We focused on support for tactical details. Every now and then, we'd also hop on the mic and promote civic engagement.

And now Strategy for Black Lives is one of the leading organizing groups not only in New York City, but in the whole Black Lives movement nationwide.

CHAPTER 8

Repeal

Tim and I were driving to Albany. We left very early, and I was tired. It was a three-hour trip from Brooklyn, so I settled in and napped while Tim drove. Partway through the ride, I woke up with a start. I'd just remembered that Tim and I had agreed to do a video interview with the *Daily Mail,* a newsgroup out of London. During that time everyone was protesting, there were constant interviews happening. Press was at an all-time high, and Strategy for Black Lives was in demand. I rigged a tripod and a light in the front seat of the car and pulled myself together just as the anchor called us. I did my best to hold the camera straight, but it was pretty clear that we were talking from a moving vehicle.

"We are on our way to Albany to support the Safer New York Act," I explained. "For us, phase one is the action of making our voices heard. Now we are moving on to phase two, where we start including civic engagement. We always stress voting dates, primaries, and filling out the census."

Strategy for Black Lives approaches Black liberation from multiple angles. In the beginning we were protesting almost every single day, but we also focused our efforts elsewhere. In the beginning we were pretty much the only organization at protests and actions that would constantly emphasize the need for people to register to vote and to fill out the census. We advocated for community-based solutions like mutual aid, political education, and civic engagement.

As an organization, we've helped young people get elected to various local government positions. We fight against gun violence, poverty, and discrimination in health, medicine, and education systems, and we work with all types of groups. We work with faith leaders, community advocates, elected officials, organizers, people on the ground. As long as they are willing to fight toward equity, we will work with them to achieve a future and a society that we deserve. Not only are we protesters and active in the street, we're also politically engaged. We call our local, state, and national representatives; we speak with public officials.

There are big issues in New York State with police violating citizens' rights, as well as with existing complaints regarding officers' individual behavior. At the time, New York had a law called 50-a that protected police officer conduct records. Repealing it was a very important first step in addressing police brutality and corruption. This would expose police officers' disciplinary records to the public. A lot of times officers guilty of targeting and attacking Black folks have multiple allegations, infractions, and complaints against them. If their bad conduct and their malicious behaviors were made public, it would be more likely that these police officers would be held accountable. They would not be allowed to repeatedly abuse people and take Black lives.

During one of our Strategy for Black Lives meetings, it was brought up that elected officials were considering passing a reform package of bills called the Safer

New York Act. One of the bills would repeal 50-a. We wanted to lend our voices to their efforts and have them speak directly to some young people. We decided to organize a trip to Albany and meet with as many legislators as possible. It was important to pick a day when the legislators were going to potentially vote on the act. Once we had that information, we could organize cars and other logistics.

When we arrived in Albany it was hot and humid. We split up into different groups and began to get to work. A lot of us have backgrounds as student leaders. Because we had lobbied legislators as student leaders for more funding for our public universities, we had the personal connections to approach them and speak to them face-to-face. We began meeting with various legislators and telling them our experiences as Black people interacting with cops. Following that, we held a press conference calling for the repeal of 50-a, and basically just voicing our position on the issue.

The state assemblyman who represented Harlem was there, Al Taylor. I'd spent a lot of time working with him while I was in the student government at my university, the City College of New York. He joked with me, but he also applauded our efforts in terms of reaching out and lobbying. He told me to "stay focused, keep fighting the good fight, apply pressure to elected officials, and capitalize on the pressure that's going on in the world to try and get some meaningful policy change."

He also told me what he thought the governor would do about the Safer New York Act.

The elected officials voted to pass the Safer New York Act that day, and a few days later the governor signed the act into law. This meant that 50-a had been repealed. Police officers no longer have sealed conduct records in the state of New York.

The news was welcome, and I was happy, but I felt like it was just one piece. Repealing

50-a is great because of the exposure of police officers' behaviors, but accountability has always been the main goal. My feeling was: *All right, cool, now we know who's horrible. On to the next goal.*

CHAPTER 9

Batman

Sometimes I feel like Batman. People often know my identity as an organizer, but they don't know that I'm a former student body president or that I'm working at a big law firm. They don't know that as a middle schooler I competed in oratory competitions or that I was president of my high school's first-ever Black Student Union.

Organizing is something that I enjoy doing. I enjoy fighting for a cause. Now that protesting has died down a bit, I'm studying for the LSAT so I can go to a top law school. I'm also working at a law firm. I think of my organizing work as parallel to the work I'm doing now. Eventually these two worlds are going to intertwine for me. To make the change that I want to make in the world, I need to go through these steps. I'm moving to the next stage of my life where my activism will take a different form.

I want to be a lawyer, but eventually I would like to become a judge. Right now, there's a huge lack of Black judges in the United States. Only around two percent of judges are Black. Judges have a lot of power. For example, within the federal penal code system they can decide that they are not going to grant a prosecutor's wish of a twenty-year sentence. Having control in that arena and being able to effect change directly in court is the way that I am planning to effect change in the criminal justice system as a whole.

I believe all my work thus far has led me to where I am today. Because of my role in the Black Student Union, I was sent to a leadership program that summer. And because of that leadership program, I was eventually on a council with the Department of Education fighting for education policy and equity. And because of that council, I became involved with IntegrateNYC, which was my first big organization. When I went to college, those skills helped me run for a position in student government and become the president. And because of that, my activism continued after I graduated, with Strategy for Black Lives.

I believe in God. I feel like God has a plan for everybody. In 2018, I was given the honor of introducing Representative John Lewis, a civil rights hero who inspired me with his life and with his words. Three years later, in April 2021, all my work came full circle. My organization Strategy for Black Lives received the John Lewis Good Trouble Award from the National Action Network. It meant a lot because it was recognition of the work that I've done over the last year in his memory. I never would have predicted in 2018 that things would look this way. But it shows that when I got the chance to meet John Lewis, his words impacted me. They stick with me every single day. Good trouble means that if you really do want to make change, you have to be comfortable with the uncomfortable. You have to be willing to step up.

Being comfortable with the uncomfortable has been the organizing principle of my entire life. If I think about the beginning of the Black Student Union, when they announced my name as president, people laughed and teased me. It was uncomfortable, but I understood that it was necessary to get where I needed to go. I didn't let it faze me. I didn't let it make me quit. I just had to get comfortable being uncomfortable, because I knew I was making change. And that's something I carry with me. Leading a movement, starting an organization, is very hard and can get very depressing at times. It's a huge burden but someone has to shoulder it. And the way I look at it is if I don't do it, then who will? I have to do my part, and hopefully it inspires other people to do their part. If everyone's doing their part to make the world a better and more equitable place, then we'll absolutely get where we need to be.

Continue the Discussion

How did the library impact Frantzy's life?

Frantzy's story of activism is deeply rooted in the libraries of Flatbush and Canarsie, where he had the opportunity to read endlessly. The library was his childhood sanctuary. There, he could explore the worlds and voices of talented authors. His afternoons reading gave him the time and opportunity to hone and distill his own voice. As his voice developed, so did his comfort with language, giving him the tools necessary for oratory competitions. His oratorical gifts blossomed into a talent for public speaking and leadership that served him as president of both the Black Student Union of his high school and of the City College student body, and later as a cofounder of Strategy for Black Lives.

How did the protests of the George Floyd murder affect New York City and the rest of the United States?

In the summer of 2020, following the murder of George Floyd by police officer Derek Chauvin, protests erupted across the United States in more than two thousand cities amid the global coronavirus pandemic. These protests in support of Black Lives continued throughout the year, spreading to over sixty countries. The movement sparked grassroots organizing and the formation of organizations such as Strategy for Black Lives. These organizations and young activists engaged the public and led the discourse on issues concerning policing and racial justice. Ultimately, their work inspired movements demanding to defund the police and invest money at the community level. They also influenced numerous legislative proposals on federal, state, and municipal levels.

In New York City, the protests led to the Safer New York Act. Among other things, the Safer New York Act repealed 50-a, a law that allowed police officer conduct records to remain sealed. As a result of the repeal, New York City police officer records are now open, allowing the public to identify officers with multiple complaints against them.

What is Frantzy doing now?

Frantzy is living at his childhood home in Flatbush and continues to be an active participant in his community. He was appointed to sit on Brooklyn Community Board 17, where he heads the Sanitation Committee and is active in enrolling other youth leaders to sit on neighborhood community boards. He continues to foster student leaders through Strategy for Black Lives and recently announced the recipients of the first Strategy for Black Lives scholarship fund. He is currently studying for the LSAT and intends to take his activism to a new level through a career in law.

Why is Strategy for Black Lives such an important part of activism?

Two days after the Zoom call that began Strategy for Black Lives, Frantzy and Timothy attended the Barclays protest in New York City. While the protest was an emotive and powerful response to the murder of George Floyd, Frantzy noted that there were things occurring at the protest that did not necessarily honor and uplift the memory of George Floyd. There was an element of cohesion missing. The protest's message was getting lost in the mayhem of the protest itself. Frantzy realized that in order to effect the change he and his peers wanted and to keep the movement's message on point, Strategy for Black Lives would need to create a framework for the organization's activism. Strategy needed a strategy. They decided to attack the issue of police brutality in phases: Phase one was the action of making their voices heard through protest and tactical support at those protests. Phase two was civic engagement. This not only focused their work but directed their energies and expertise toward venues where they could be of particular use. Those with oratory gifts could petition legislators to repeal legislation like 50-a, while those with tactical experience could lead support at protests. Because of the plans and strategy they put into play, Frantzy's organization was able to make a more effective impact.

Get Involved

1. Empower.

Encourage others to find their voice. Whatever a person is passionate about, support their efforts to speak up and reach their goals. Extend gratitude and positivity toward them, and believe in yourself and your ideals in the same way.

2. Educate.

Be willing to learn. Remember that "a wise man knows nothing." Be equally willing to unlearn toxic practices in order to grow.

Read anti-racist literature, listen to podcasts that discuss race studies, and attend events in your community that help you continually better understand these issues.

3. Enact.

Be bold and courageous in fighting for the changes you seek from the world. Contact your elected officials. Organize your friends. March and protest. Live the values you believe. Everyone is capable, and no goal is too ambitious as long as you believe in yourself and the work.

Timeline

2010

Mrs. Dupre identifies Frantzy's skill with language in sixth grade, and encourages him to enter oratory competitions, which he does the next year, in 2011.

2014

At the age of fifteen, Frantzy and his friend Patrick attend their first protest after the murder of Eric Garner on July 17.

2012-2016

Frantzy begins attending a predominantly white high school. Faced with microaggressions and ignorance from white students, Frantzy helps found the Black Student Union. As president of the Black Student Union, he organizes events and outreach in an effort to help make the school environment better and more equitable for its Black students and students of color.

Fall 2016

Frantzy begins his college journey at the City College of New York with a focus in political

science. He finds friendship and brotherhood in the fraternity Alpha Phi Alpha and
is elected student body president.

August 2018

Frantzy attends the first International
Congress of Youth Voices and is privileged
with the opportunity to introduce civil rights
icon Congressman John Lewis.

March 2020

Covid-19 emerges as a deadly and unimag-
inably contagious disease in the United States,

causing upheaval and illness throughout the country and the world.

May 25, 2020

George Floyd is murdered by police officer Derek Chauvin and the incident is filmed by a civilian. As people sit trapped in their homes by the Covid-19 pandemic, the video goes viral, sparking protest and activism globally.

May 26, 2020

Frantzy organizes a Zoom call with young leaders in response to the murder of George Floyd. Together, the group of activists creates a list of seven demands in reaction to police violence and presents the demands at a press conference the following day.

On May 29, Frantzy marches in the infamous New York City Barclays protest and realizes that the movement for Black Lives will need strategy and a multipronged approach in order to thrive and foment change.

June 1, 2020

People peacefully protesting police brutality in Washington, D.C.'s Lafayette Square are violently tear-gassed to allow President Trump to walk through the square in service of a photo opportunity.

Summer 2020

Protests erupt across the globe in support of Black Lives Matter. Frantzy's organization Strategy for Black Lives begins attending protests and actions, offering tactical and strategic assistance.

April 2021

Frantzy's activism comes full circle, and he is honored with the John Lewis Good Trouble Award for his work with Strategy for Black Lives.

Author's Acknowledgments

First and foremost, all praise is due to the Most High. I am truly blessed to have lived such a life and must give thanks to God.

I would not be here without the support of my family: my mom Marilyne, my dad Frantz, and my older brother Ted. Thank you for raising me to become the person that I am today. And to my grandma, Mamita. Te amo y te extraño.

I would like to acknowledge the editorial team Amanda Uhle, Zainab Nasrati, Zoe Rosenblum, Zoë Ruiz, and Dave Eggers, for all their hard work in bringing this book to life. I would also like to acknowledge the

International Congress of Youth Voices and its community of activists, change-makers, and creatives. The relationships I have built through this community are truly priceless.

To Ms. Dupre and Ms. Tercious (may God rest her soul), who recognized my God-given gifts as early as middle school. Thank you, and sorry for always reading non-school books in class.

To my day one Patrick, who bore witness firsthand to everything described in this book from the beginning to the present. Thank you.

To Maurice Blackmon and Sarah Camiscoli, whose mentorship and guidance have been invaluable. I can say without hesitation that I would not be any sort of leader, activist, or organizer without you. You both are perfect examples of what it means to invest in and acknowledge youth voice and leadership. Thank you.

To Leon M. Goldstein's Black Student Union and Respect for All community, to Ms. Rogers, to Ms. Shaker, to Ms. Arciniegas, to Coro's Inaugural Youth Leadership Academy, and to Rahmel. Thank you.

To my IntegrateNYC family, the foundation of my activism, thank you for all the lessons learned, the lifelong friends, and the ability to inspire so many youths across New York City.

To Iman, my activist partner in crime, thank you.

To my people from the City College of New York, especially my team at the Undergraduate Student Government, and the student leaders all across the City University of New York and the University Student Senate, thank you for an amazing four years. Special thanks to Ali and the Macaulay Honors Program.

To the brothers of Eta "the Jewel" Chapter of Alpha Phi Alpha Fraternity, Inc. You all helped me grow exponentially as a Black man and I am always grateful to the brotherhood. Life is hard.

To Jaret, a.k.a. J$, thank you for always putting up with my shenanigans and being a trusted confidant.

To Strategy for Black Lives, a team that

I will forever be proud of, to the entire New York organizing community, and to all my comrades and accomplices who fought alongside us within this era of the movement and will continue to do so, thank you. It's a strategy.

To Trenae, for all your endless love and support, thank you.

To my "4Liferss," Delano, Bryan, and Tyler, thank you for always believing in the vision. You already know this is just the beginning.

To all of my friends, peers, colleagues, and anyone who's ever supported or impacted me, no matter the size, throughout my twenty-three years on this planet. Thank you.

AUTHOR'S ACKNOWLEDGMENTS

Thank you to the communities of East Flatbush, Canarsie, all of Brooklyn, the city of New York, my Haitian brothers and sisters, and the entire African diaspora who have poured into me.

This book is a by-product of all the aforementioned and I will do everything in my power to pay it forward.

Editors' Acknowledgments

The editors would like to extend special thanks to the Young Editors Project (YEP), which connects young readers to manuscripts in progress. The program gives meaningful opportunities for young people to be part of the professional publishing process and gives authors and publishers meaningful insights into their work. Special thanks to Kristin Allard, Simon Boughton, Nyuol Lueth Tong, Zoë Ruiz, Anika Hussain, Isabella Dixon, Ashley Peterson, Corinne Licardo, and Ilaria Degrassi.

www.youngeditorsproject.org

About I, Witness

I, Witness is a nonfiction book series that tells important stories of real young people who have faced and conquered extraordinary contemporary challenges. There's no better way for young readers to learn about the world's issues and upheavals than through the eyes of young people who have lived through these times.

Proceeds from this book series support the work of the International Alliance of Youth Writing Centers and its sixty-plus member organizations. These nonprofit writing centers are joined in a common belief that young people need places where they can write and be heard, where they can have their voices celebrated and amplified.

www.youthwriting.org